Growing Up in
Russia

Other titles in the *Growing Up Around the World* series include:

Growing Up in
Russia

James Roland

San Diego, CA

© 2018 ReferencePoint Press, Inc.
Printed in the United States

For more information, contact:
ReferencePoint Press, Inc.
PO Box 27779
San Diego, CA 92198
www. ReferencePointPress.com

LIBRARY OF CONGRESS CATALOGING-IN-PUBLICATION DATA

Name: Roland, James, author.
Title: Growing Up in Russia/by James Roland.
Description: San Diego, CA: ReferencePoint Press, [2017] | Series: Growing
  Up Around the World | Audience: Grade 9 to 12. | Includes bibliographical
  references and index.
Identifiers: LCCN 2016056741 (print) | LCCN 2017010936 (ebook) | ISBN
  9781682822234 (hardback) | ISBN 9781682822241 (eBook)
Subjects: LCSH: Russia (Federation)--Social conditions--Juvenile literature.
  | Russia (Federation)--Social life and customs--Juvenile literature. |
  Families--Russia (Federation)--Juvenile literature.
Classification: LCC HN530.2.A8 R586 2017 (print) | LCC HN530.2.A8 (ebook) |
  DDC 306.0947--dc23
LC record available at https://lccn.loc.gov/2016056741

CONTENTS

Official Name
Russian Federation (commonly known as Russia)

Size
6,592,772 sq. miles
(17,075,200 sq. km)

Total Population
143,436,633 as of 2016

Youth Population
0–14 years: 16.4%
15–24 years: 10.07%

Religions
Orthodox Christian: 72%
Muslim: 5%
Catholic, Protestant, Jewish, and Buddhist: 1% each

Capital
Moscow

Type of Government
Semipresidential republic

Language
Russian

Currency
Ruble

Industries
Petroleum and mining, machine and vehicle production, textiles

Literacy
99.7% (age 15+ able to read and write)

Internet Users
102.3 million, or 71.3% of population

7

CHAPTER ONE

The Country and Its People

Russia, known officially as the Russian Federation, is a vast nation that stretches from eastern Europe to the Pacific Ocean. It is a land of mountains and farmland; oil fields, seaports, and factories; railways and highways. Its people live in bustling cities, tiny villages, and a wide range of places in between. The many distinct geographic regions and cultural differences ensure that young people in one part of the country will likely have very different experiences growing up from young people in other parts of the country.

These differences clearly stand out when looking at two youth populations—one in the capital city of Moscow and another that is more than 3,000 miles (4,828 km) away on the Yamal Peninsula in northern Siberia. Students attending Moscow High School No. 548, in the southern part of Russia's capital, spend a portion of their day in state-of-the-art computer labs as part of an international education program sponsored by Microsoft. They wear jeans and hoodies or sweaters. After school, students hang out at a local café or park before heading home for a few hours of homework. This experience differs markedly from that of the young people who are growing up near the Arctic Circle. These young people, members of a nomadic and indigenous people known as the Nenets, spend half the year in boarding schools hundreds of miles away from home. The rest of the year, clothed in warm furs to protect against extreme cold, they help out with the family business: guiding herds of reindeer to grazing areas and then selling reindeer meat.

A Vast and Varied Landscape
Russia's geography is as wide ranging as the cultures and lifestyles of its people. Measuring almost 6.6 million square miles

(17,075,200 sq. km), Russia spans two continents (Europe and Asia) and eleven time zones. European Russia is considered to be the area that extends from the borders with Finland, Ukraine, and Belarus east to the Ural Mountains and to the border of Kazakhstan in the south. Rivers such as the Volga, a 2,193-mile-long (3,529 km) river that is the longest in Europe, wind their way through the dense forests and scattered farmlands that separate Russia's largest cities. European Russia contains the country's two most populous cities: Moscow and Saint Petersburg, as well as most of the country's education and industrial centers. European Russia comprises only about a quarter of the land area of the country but three-quarters of its population.

Asian Russia is the land that extends east from the Ural Mountains to the northern Pacific Ocean. It includes most of the land area of Russia yet only a fourth of its total population. Much of Asian Russia is known by another name—Siberia. Its economy is supported largely by mining (nickel, lead, coal, and other minerals) and the oil and natural gas industries. Farming dominates the southwestern region of Siberia. The largest city in this part of Russia is Novosibirsk, an industrial center just east of the Ural Mountains, with a population of about 1.4 million.

Asian Russia is made up mostly of flat plains known as steppes, though there are several mountain ranges primarily in the southern and northeastern regions. And across the wide expanse of northern Russia is a sparsely populated tundra. People who live there refer to the white nights, in which the sun does not set until after midnight in the summer and then rises again only a few hours later. In the winter, the reverse is true, with only a few hours of sunlight each day.

Frigid temperatures and gray skies dominate the long and dreary Russian winters across most of the country. The average winter temperatures hover around 20°F (-6.7°C), often dipping well below zero. As much as the landscape changes from east to west and north to south, Russia's notorious winters are as constant as the stars overlooking the ice and snow below. It has often been observed that Russia's brutal winter climate has helped instill a toughness in the Russian people and continually reinforced the idea that only as a group can Russians survive. Writes Gregory Feifer, a former National Public Radio correspondent and author

Pictured is a young member of the Nenets, an indigenous people who live near the Arctic Circle in northern Russia. Russia is a vast nation that spreads across many distinct geographical and cultural areas.

of *Russians: The People Behind the Power*: "Many factors have influenced the national character over several centuries, including Russia's vast territory—much of it uninhabitable—its harsh winter, its history and culture."[1]

Diverse Population

Russia's population, which numbers more than 143 million people, represents a broad array of ethnic groups—nearly two hundred in all. The largest single ethnic group is Russians, making up about 80 percent of the population. The second-biggest group is the Tatars, who live mostly in western Russia. Groups such as Ukrainians, Bashkirs, and the Chuvash also live in European Russia. In Siberia groups such as the Yakuts—nearly 250,000 strong and made up of nomadic hunters and fishers—raise cattle and breed horses. In the far northeastern corner of Siberia, several small ethnic groups still survive, including the Chuvans, who number less than 1,000. In southwestern Russia, in a region bounded by the Black Sea on the west and the Caspian Sea on the east, is an area known as the Caucasus. Dozens of different ethnic groups live within this region.

While many of these groups coexist peacefully, conflicts do arise. The Chechen people, who live in a region of the North Caucasus known as the Chechen Republic (or Chechnya), have long sought independence from Russia. Chechen and Russian differences have led to violent confrontations.

Russian nationalists have also been involved in ethnic conflicts and violence. The nationalists are ethnic Russians who see themselves as the only true Russians. They oppose the presence of immigrants (especially those who are Muslim) and other ethnic groups in their country. Russian nationalist groups are on the rise. Many of their newest converts are young people who believe their country has grown weak and has been hurt by growing numbers of ethnic populations. They take inspiration from the Cold War years from the 1940s to the early 1990s, when Russia formed the heart of the Soviet Union—which was one of the world's two superpowers.

> "Many factors have influenced the national character over several centuries, including Russia's vast territory—much of it uninhabitable—its harsh winter, its history and culture."[1]
>
> —Gregory Feifer, a former NPR correspondent and author of *Russians: The People Behind the Power*

Russia's Big Cities

Russia's youth population, in general, is shrinking. Since the early 1990s Russians have been having fewer children. Concerns about the shrinking birth rate have led the government to provide financial rewards for families that have or adopt a second child. These measures are meeting with mixed results. At present, almost 27 percent of Russia's population is age twenty-five or younger. This is still larger than the population of Russians who are sixty-five or older—a group that represents less than 14 percent.

The majority of these young people, and indeed, most of the general population, live in cities. Almost three-quarters of the population are in urban centers. Moscow is the largest, with a population of nearly 12 million people. Saint Petersburg has about 5 million residents. Both cities are in western, or European, Russia. The next two biggest cities, Novosibirsk and Yekaterinburg, are in Asian Russia.

Moscow is not just the country's capital. It is also Russia's center of business, education and culture. Though Moscow is densely populated—most people live in multistory apartment buildings—and there is a lot of traffic, it is actually one of the greener cities of its size anywhere in the world. Nearly one hundred parks and eighteen public gardens break up the sea of buildings and roads. Along with the 170 square miles (440 sq. km) devoted to green space, Moscow contains nearly 40 square miles (104 sq. km) of forests. The parks come alive, especially on weekends, with

A group of teenagers sits on a bench in Moscow. Since the early 1990s the Russian youth population has been shrinking as people have been having fewer children.

music festivals and sporting events. The parks also draw young people and families to relax in tranquil surroundings, a nice break from work and school.

Unlike landlocked Moscow, Saint Petersburg is a busy port city on the Baltic Sea. The Neva River snakes through the city, providing beautiful views of the city's architectural gems. More so than Moscow, Saint Petersburg has retained much of its centuries-old churches and royal buildings. Interestingly, though, Saint Petersburg is also one of the more Westernized cities in Russia. It is Russia's hub for a growing high-tech industry, and the city is the home of many manufacturing plants associated with international companies, such as Ford and Toyota. The city's new glass and steel buildings seem somehow to fit in alongside the historic palaces, churches, and ornate bridges across the gray-blue waterways that slice through Saint Petersburg.

Russia prides itself on excellence in the arts and athletics. The cities offer many options for those inclined to take part in these activities. Live theater, cinemas, symphonies, ballet, sporting events, and other forms of entertainment can be found in most cities.

Russia's Rural Lands

Far fewer entertainment options exist in the rural areas that make up most of the country. Indeed, there are fewer options for some of life's basic necessities in rural Russia. Many small towns used to be thriving communities built around factories. For example, in the town of Bryansk—a six-hour train ride from Moscow and once home to massive steel mills and locomotive production plants—manufacturing has largely disappeared. Poverty has overtaken Bryansk and many similar communities. About 13 percent of Russian children grow up in poverty, most of them in rural areas. In any direction from a major city, the landscape often turns sad and bleak. Villages of fewer than one hundred people, many of them living in poorly insulated shacks, dot the countryside from the western hill country to the plains of Siberia.

Some villages are prospering. These might have successful privately owned farms or small corporate farms. Mines filled with precious metals, as well as oil and natural gas fields, are also keeping some rural areas going. But rural villages that are not supported by farming, mining, or other industries are disappearing off the map. The town of Zimnitsy, for instance, has ten residents. The little spot six hours north of Moscow no longer has enough people to support a shop. Instead, a green goods truck pulls into the middle of town periodically, and Zimnitsy's few inhabitants line up to buy fish, sausages, cabbage, and whatever other items happen to be available.

Some rural areas, particularly those in scenic forested regions, provide spaces for the vacation homes of wealthy city dwellers. Dachas, or country homes, serve as getaways for Muscovites and others who wish to escape the crowded cities. City dwellers who head to the country on weekends or for extended holidays are called Dachniki. They tend to build new cottages or renovate old ones. The dacha has been a popular retreat for Russia's upper classes for more than two hundred years.

A Complicated Past

Russia has been through remarkable changes in recent decades. Many long-held Russian family traditions continue today, and the shadow of a century of Communist rule still lingers.

Up until 1918, Russia was like many European countries. It had an aristocracy and was led by a family that had ruled for generations. Russia's equivalent of a king was called a czar. Economic, social, and political turmoil spread across Russia in the first part of the twentieth century, leading to the takeover of the government by the Communist Party. Communists created the Union of Soviet Socialist Republics (USSR, also known as the Soviet Union), and Russia was at the center of this new nation. Over subsequent decades, the Soviet Union added to its territory by taking control of Ukraine, Belarus, Georgia, and other bordering regions. After World War II, Moscow extended its influence over countries in Eastern Europe, such as Poland, East Germany, Romania, and Hungary.

Life in the Soviet Union was difficult for many people. Food and basic goods were not always easily available. There was little opportunity to improve one's station in life. Suspected enemies of the government were often jailed or killed. The central government limited freedoms and exerted control over much of society. Religion was essentially outlawed, and most Russians were prohibited from moving to other countries. Young people

A Very Long Train

One way to grasp the size of Russia and its incredibly varied landscape is to take the Trans-Siberian Railway. It spans almost the entire width of the country, and at 5,700 miles (9,173 km) of track, it is the longest railway in the world. To ride from Moscow to the major Pacific port city of Vladivostok—the railway's two endpoints—takes more than 152 hours (or a little more than six full days). Private berths and delicious meals are available. Among the interesting stops along the way are Baikalsk, a major ski and snowboard destination; Krasnoyarsk, a scenic region for canoeing and hiking; and Irkutsk, home to several universities and a fun town for young people. The Trans-Siberian Railway is used mainly to carry goods from factories to the cities. But it always has plenty of passengers: college students going to and from school, Russians visiting relatives, businesspeople traveling for their jobs, and many tourists from abroad. The railway also includes international lines that take passengers through Mongolia and past the Great Wall of China all the way to Beijing.

were steered into jobs on the basis of the government's view of what was needed, rather than being able to pursue their own interests. Kids who showed athletic prowess were sent to academies, often far from home, with hopes they would bring Olympic glory to the USSR.

In the early 1980s, political, economic, and social changes were taking hold throughout Soviet society. As the Soviet Union's economy faltered in the late 1980s and more progressive leaders assumed powerful positions in the government, it became clear that huge changes were on the horizon. Younger leaders embraced ideas such as perestroika (restructuring) and glasnost (openness). Unable to sustain its economy and political system, the USSR disbanded in 1991. Ukraine and several other former members of the USSR regained their independence. Russia reorganized as the Russian Federation.

Government

Russia's seat of government is a fortified complex of buildings in Moscow called the Kremlin. The Kremlin has housed a variety of political and military leaders since the fourteenth century. In addition to the offices of the federal government, the Kremlin is also the residence of Russia's president.

The Russian Federation functions as a semipresidential republic. It has two leaders: a president and a prime minister, though the president has more power than the prime minister. The president is considered the head of state, while the prime minister oversees more of the day-to-day operations of the government. Russia has had this type of government since 1993. The legislative branch of the Russian government is called the Federal Assembly. It is made up of a 178-seat Federal Council and a 450-seat State Duma. A Russian citizen can run for a seat on the Duma starting at age twenty-one. The Duma has elected representatives from twenty-one Russian Republics and sixty-six independent regions and territories. The republics mostly represent areas throughout the country dominated by non-Russian ethnic groups. The independent regions and territories are more representative of Russia's majority population. Each of these republics and territories also has its own leaders and legislative bodies, though the responsibilities and authority of local governments tend to change often.

Rich Cultural Traditions

This fascinating country also has an amazing cultural history. Classical music, ballet, literature, art, and architecture are all part of the fabric of Russia. Russia counts among its most famous sons and daughters authors Leo Tolstoy (*War and Peace*) and Fyodor Dostoevsky (*Crime and Punishment*), composers Pyotr Tchaikovsky (*The Nutcracker*) and Nikolai Rimsky-Korsakov (*Scheherazade*), ballet dancers Anna Pavlova and Mikhail Baryshnikov, artists Wassily Kandinsky and Natalia Goncharova, as well as poet Alexander Pushkin, playwright Anton Chekhov, and countless others in the visual and performing arts

> "We may not love practice, but we all love ballet."[2]
>
> —Nikolai "Kolya" Chevuichalov, a seventeen-year-old dance student in Moscow

Folk arts also have a rich tradition in Russia. There is a sweetness and beauty in Russia's famous nesting dolls (or *matryoshka* dolls), in which a wooden painted doll hides a similar, but smaller version of itself inside. And inside that second doll is a smaller ver-

sion, and so on. The intricately painted dolls traditionally depicted a peasant woman, but more modern versions include historical figures, political leaders, and other characters.

The arts continue to be an important part of life for many young people in Russia. The schools make visual and performing arts a part of the daily curriculum, and children are encouraged at a young age to take up a musical instrument or dance. "We may not love practice, but we all love ballet,"[2] says Nikolai "Kolya" Chevuichalov, a seventeen-year-old dance student in Moscow. Viktoria "Vika" Mishukova, a ten-year-old at the same dance school, is like many young girls of Russia who dream of becoming a famous ballerina. "It's pretty hard," she says. "But I like the beauty of dance, the grace, the lightness. And I love all the jumping."[3]

Those who do not pursue the arts often find a sport they enjoy. Russia has a long history of success in the Winter and Summer Olympics, as well as other athletic endeavors.

Life in Russia Not So Different

For young people growing up in Russia, family, school, sports, arts, chores, friendships, dating, and countless other activities make their lives much like those of youths in other countries. Still, an oppressive government and economic hardships are part of everyday life for many young Russians. Freedom of expression is limited in many ways, such as the censorship of Internet content and the persecution of the lesbian, gay, bisexual, and transgen-

Growing Up and Blasting Off

The dream of traveling in space is one shared by many young people in Russia, the country that first broke the barrier between Earth and the cosmos. One of the Soviet Union's proudest accomplishments is having been the first nation to launch a satellite into orbit around the Earth and to put a man in space. Today Russia continues to be one of the main partners in the International Space Station. After some difficult years that included many delays in the construction of a $3 billion space center in eastern Russia, the nation that first sent a human being into space is hoping to once again be a leader in the space industry. Russia has plans to build a base on the moon, after making its first scheduled lunar landing in 2031.

Russia's space program, known as Roscosmos, is making a concerted effort to recruit young people to pursue engineering careers in space technology. An estimated 110,000 space specialists are needed by 2025, Roscosmos says. The need for young talent is based partly on the ambitious plans for the next few decades and partly on the fact that many of the engineers currently working for Roscosmos are older veterans of the Soviet space program. Roscosmos is promising good-paying jobs and the excitement that comes from being part of the lunar missions and the other goals for Russia's next chapter in its ongoing space saga.

der (LGBT) community. Many Russian parents struggle to afford simple things such as new shoes and school clothes for their children.

And yet many Russian youths have plenty of the amenities of twenty-first-century life: a smartphone, video games, a laptop computer, and stylish clothes. Innovations in technology, music, fashion, and politics are just as much a part of life for many Russian youths as they are for kids in the United States. For example, S. Elliott Estebo, an American who taught English in Russia and later worked on international cultural and educational programs for the American Councils for International Education, says the most surprising thing American teens noticed when they spent time in Russia is how similar life is for kids in both countries. He explains:

> "Our societies [US and Russian] are, in many ways, more similar than people, including teens, in either country realize. . . . There really is no 'typical American teen' or 'typical Russian teen.'"[4]
>
> —S. Elliott Estebo, an American who taught English in Russia

Our societies are, in many ways, more similar than people, including teens, in either country realize. Both countries have huge multinational, multicultural, and multi-religious societies, so there really is no "typical American teen" or "typical Russian teen." . . . Regardless of where they are from, most teens in both countries have the same concerns: fitting in at school, seeing the newest movies, and spending time with friends.[4]

CHAPTER TWO

Home and Family

It is dinnertime in Saint Petersburg, and around the family table are a mother, a father, two children, and a grandmother who just finished making her delicious beef stroganoff and potatoes. Everyone drinks hot tea, perhaps flavored with orange, lemon, or spices. The conversation starts with what the kids did in school that day and eventually turns to plans for New Year's Day festivities and the impending ski trip with relatives in Yekaterinburg, a beautiful city near the Ural Mountains. Though most Russian families have only one or two children, family life has long been at the heart of Russian society. In hard economic and political times, family members who share a home—parents, children, and often grandparents—could find strength in each other.

Extended Families

In many Russian families, both husbands and wives work outside the home. In families with children, the burden of caring for children often falls to grandparents—especially grandmothers. But this is usually a happy burden for grandparents and their families. In fact, many grandmothers retire from their own jobs to spend time helping once their first grandchild is born.

Because grandparents are so involved in raising children in Russia, grandparents and grandchildren often form close bonds. This is especially true of the grandmother, or in Russian, *babushka*. When a student comes home with an excellent grade or some other accomplishment in school, often the first person who hears the news is the babushka. In countless Russian families, the grandmother is the heart and soul of the home, and therefore a very cherished person in Russian society. Tatiana Golubeva, a Moscow native and marketing executive who also blogs about everyday life in Russia, says:

> Grandparents, and especially grandmothers, play key parts in families. They spend time with grandchildren, often replacing nannies. We do not have babysitters in Russia. You either have a nanny or a grandmother is doing the nanny's work. For so many families that is crucial, as they cannot afford a paid nanny. Also, people think that a grandmother is better than a nanny. And for grandmothers, it is actually a joy to feel needed and spend time with grandchildren.[5]

Mealtime in Russia

A Russian home with a grandmother usually means plenty of traditional meals. Even though fast-food options are more available in many Russian cities and towns than ever before, most families still prefer home-cooked meals. Russians also tend to have more than the standard three meals a day. Lighter meals or snacks are a part of a typical Russian's diet. A student might have a breakfast of eggs and sausage at home and then a midmorning meal at school of porridge, for example, and then lunch (often called dinner in Russia). A 4:00 p.m. snack of mini sandwiches, scones, or other light items with tea, similar to teatime in the United Kingdom, is a long-standing tradition. It is an important one, since the evening meal tends to be later on weekdays. That is because in most families both parents work, so getting home and then making supper puts mealtime close to 7:30 p.m. in many households. When a babushka is available to prepare dinner, kids and parents may not have to wait so long for their evening meal. A lot of Russian teenagers make after-school stops at McDonald's and other fast-food restaurants to tide themselves over until dinner. There are more than five hundred McDonald's restaurants in Russia, including the largest one in Europe, located at Pushkin Square in Moscow.

Traditional Russian meals often start with soup. One of the most popular—and traditional—is borscht, a sour beet soup.

Some classic Russian entrees include smoked salmon, salted herring, *pelmeni* (meat-filled dumplings), and shashlik (shish kebabs of beef, lamb, or chicken served with Russian pickles and a spicy tomato sauce). Coffee or hot tea is served at most meals, and these beverages tend to be stronger than those same beverages served in other countries.

When a Russian family gathers around the table for supper, the meal can last a long time. The conversation and stories flow, especially when other relatives or guests are included. Russians are fond of toasts; a single meal might include many toasts, which are usually long and include a story. Food served to visitors is usually extra special as a sign of hospitality. Visitors to a Russian family's home usually arrive with a gift such as wine or chocolate.

The warmth and affection that surrounds supper in a Russian home often starts as the meal is being prepared, according to

People line up to order a quick meal from a McDonald's in Moscow. While most Russian families prepare and cook meals at home, many teenagers grab snacks at fast-food restaurants after school to tide themselves over until dinner.

Aleksandra Efimova, a Russian food writer and blogger for Russia Beyond the Headlines. In a 2016 blog post, she writes:

> I remember from my childhood in St. Petersburg that eating was central. No matter how many family members or guests were in the house, they all seemed to end up in the kitchen. To this day, I'm not sure how they all fit; the kitchen in the first house I remember was only five square meters in size (about 50 square feet). Our next kitchen was a couple of square meters larger, but still very small, and it's hard to believe how many people would squeeze into such a tiny area. But squeeze into it they did, because the kitchen is truly the heart of the Russian home. Everyone gravitates to the kitchen and they can sit for hours around the table, enjoying a meal together but also sharing conversation, stories, jokes and songs.[6]

Apartment Living

A cozy home and vibrant family life can help make up for the cramped quarters of most Russian apartments. Block after block of five- or six-story gray apartment buildings fill the landscapes of Russia's cities. Many of them were built in the 1960s and 1970s, when the Soviets guaranteed everyone housing, but not necessarily luxurious accommodations. As available real estate became scarce in Moscow and other cities, taller apartment buildings were constructed.

The typical Russian apartment has a narrow corridor with a coat rack, shoe rack, and mirror. The apartment's one bathroom is just off the corridor. The average kitchen is only about 18 square feet (1.7 sq. m) in size, but it is the heart of the home. As dinner is being prepared, guests often gather in the kitchen rather than in the more spacious living room. The living room is about 50 to 60 square feet

> "The kitchen is truly the heart of the Russian home. Everyone gravitates to the kitchen and they can sit for hours around the table, enjoying a meal together but also sharing conversation, stories, jokes and songs."[6]
>
> —Aleksandra Efimova, a food blogger and native of Saint Petersburg, Russia

(4.6 to 5.6 sq. m). It is not unusual for a family member to use the living room sofa as a bed, since there are usually only one or two bedrooms in an average Russian apartment. Most apartments have a small balcony that looks out at other apartment buildings. With limited space inside, the balconies are often used for storage.

Nearly three-quarters of Russia's population live in cities or nearby suburbs. Neighborhoods made up of identical-looking apartment complexes—called microdistricts or microrayons—provide Russian youths with a common bond. Generation after generation of Russian kids can tell similarly sad, sometimes nostalgic, stories of growing up in these featureless neighborhoods. Anastasiia Fedorova, a writer who grew up in a suburb of Saint Petersburg, wrote a feature in the *Guardian* newspaper describing a return to the neighborhood where she grew up:

> Building 8 is exactly the same as building 14, and its young inhabitants must perhaps have the same preoccupation: to someday acquire a similar cell in one of these purpose-built units around town. . . . The suburbs are the best reflection of Russian life—vast and meaningless, ugly and violent, littered with scrap metal and plastic bags. But also full of melancholy beauty during a radiant chemical pink sunset. This is our ugly, mean and elusive Arcadia [a utopian region in Greek mythology]—impossible to find and impossible to leave.[7]

Rural Homes

Away from the city's endless apartment buildings and busy streets, Russia's landscape is peppered with villages, farms, and small towns. If a family has a farm that sustains them or they live in a thriving town, they may live in a one- or two-story wooden house that is much more spacious than a city apartment. While a rural home can be comfortable, especially in the summer, the great challenge many families face is getting through a frigid Russian winter. Anna Stepanova, who was born and raised in Siberia, says some newer homes have central heating. But there are plenty of traditional little houses across Siberia that rely on a *pech* (oven) for heat as well as cooking during those brutal Siberian cold spells. "Every morning we would put coal and firewood inside, fire it up and soon the whole house would become warm," Stepanova says. "The oven worked as a cooker as well. We had an electric stove too, but let me tell you that nothing beats the taste of food cooked over the real fire!"[8]

In some of Russia's poorest rural areas, one- or two-room wooden shacks might house an entire family. On the flip side, Russia's countryside is also dotted with cozy cottages that were once dachas built for occasional use by city dwellers. In recent years some former city residents have decided to move into their dachas full time, either to escape the congestion of the cities or to avoid the increasing cost of living in an urban region.

Russia's rural landscape is peppered with villages, farms, and small towns. Rural homes are much larger and more comfortable than the cramped apartments in the cities.

Not Much Privacy

Whether they are growing up in a tiny apartment in the city or a little wooden farmhouse on the steppes, Russian youths grow up without a lot of privacy. Siblings tend to share bedrooms, and with extended families living under one roof, there are usually few places to find solitude at home. "This affects many aspects of life, including how family members relate to one another," S. Elliott Estebo says. "Russians tend not to expect to have their own personal space, whereas most American teens have their own bedrooms and may spend time there (in the home) away from family members."[9]

> "Russians tend not to expect to have their own personal space, whereas most American teens have their own bedrooms and may spend time there (in the home) away from family members."[9]
>
> —S. Elliott Estebo, an American who taught English in Russia

Even living in a dormitory at college, young Russians find their privacy is often limited. Students are expected to be in their own rooms every night rather than staying out too late or staying overnight somewhere else. Student Elena Gasyukova says attendants at her dorm at Moscow's Higher School of Economics check in on students every night at nine o'clock. "If the attendant doesn't see me for a while, she will make a note of it and report it to my parents,"[10] says Gasyukova.

Marriage and Leaving Home

Heading off to college or leaving home to pursue a career have been options for young men in Russia for a long time, but they are relatively new opportunities for young women there. For many years a Russian girl could expect to be married by the time she turned eighteen or nineteen. The average age for men to marry was only a little older.

Now that is changing. The ages for a first marriage have climbed in Russia to about twenty-seven for men and about twenty-four for women, and those ages are expected to rise in the years ahead. Couples are also delaying the age at which they have kids. It is also more common for couples either to live together before getting married or not to get married at all. One reason more young Russians are delaying marriage is to focus on careers in the country's rapidly changing economy. New tech start-ups and Russian-based companies expanding their reach into international markets are providing ambitious young people more career options than they have ever had.

Many young adults in Russia are also putting off marriage because it is hard to find a place to live and start a family. Once Russians are out of school, they may still find themselves living at home with their parents. Unlike in the Soviet era, housing is no longer guaranteed. And as more people move into the cities, apartment prices in Moscow and other urban areas are rising fast. This makes it harder for young people to afford their own places. For some young people, even those with university degrees, that means living with their parents well into their twenties.

Views of marriage among young Russians are changing in other ways as well. Tatyana Gurko, head of family sociology at the Russian Academy of Sciences' Institute of Sociology, describes a growing trend that is shaking the institution of the family in Russia. "During the past decade, the family values of young people have been starting to exclude an expectation of lifelong marriage. The new generation, including those with children of their own, has loyalties that lie with successive

Dachas: Russia's Weekend Getaway Cottages

Because many Russian families living in the cities live in small apartments, having a summer or weekend home in the countryside is a welcome and important part of family life. These second homes are called dachas. They are usually simple cottages, though wealthier families have some fairly large and elaborate dachas. An estimated 25 percent of Russian families own such a country getaway. Dachas are often located in serene wooded areas, where families can take relaxing strolls or have cookouts over an open fire. Many families plant potatoes or vegetable gardens near their dachas, since gardening is not usually an option for city living. In tough economic times, some families give up their city apartments and make their dachas their year-round home. For generations of young people in Russia, the dacha is often part of cherished childhood memories.

The age for marriage has climbed in Russia and is expected to continue to rise in the years ahead. Many young people are choosing to delay marriage to focus on their careers.

marriages, children out of wedlock, cohabitation with unmarried partners, and even infidelity."[11] Today about half of Russia's marriages end in divorce. It has one of the highest divorce rates of any developed nation on earth.

Family and Holiday Activities

Amid all the changes, however, there still remains a current of traditional family life that persists in many homes across Russia. In the evenings children may practice their musical instruments or play video games or spend time engaged with social media. Watching TV with the family is also a common evening activity. Chess is something of a national obsession in Russia, so it is not uncommon to find a parent and child engrossed in a game of chess after dinner.

Families also do a lot of outdoor activities together. During the bitterly cold winters, they might go skiing or sledding. In warmer months bicycling is becoming popular. Big cities such as Moscow have few bike lanes, but the government is adding more bicycle trails in the capital's parks, and these are popular with families.

Live theater is extremely popular in Russia. Families with younger kids have many children's theater options, including the Moscow Cat Theater, which features trained cats that do acrobatics and other tricks. Teens and their parents regularly take in plays, operas, and ballets at the Mariinsky Opera and Ballet Theater and the Alexandrinsky Theater, both in Saint Petersburg. The world-famous Bolshoi Theatre, which is in many ways the national theater of Russia, puts on amazing new ballet, opera, and other theatrical productions while also preserving musical theater history.

When not enjoying a musical or dramatic performance in the theater, many Russian families tend to make mealtime a produc-

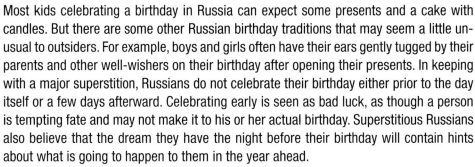

Happy Birthday! Let Me Pull Your Ears!

Most kids celebrating a birthday in Russia can expect some presents and a cake with candles. But there are some other Russian birthday traditions that may seem a little unusual to outsiders. For example, boys and girls often have their ears gently tugged by their parents and other well-wishers on their birthday after opening their presents. In keeping with a major superstition, Russians do not celebrate their birthday either prior to the day itself or a few days afterward. Celebrating early is seen as bad luck, as though a person is tempting fate and may not make it to his or her actual birthday. Superstitious Russians also believe that the dream they have the night before their birthday will contain hints about what is going to happen to them in the year ahead.

Birthday parties are usually held at the home of the person celebrating the big day, though in recent years teens and adults are starting to have birthday celebrations in restaurants and other locations outside the home. At parties for younger Russian kids, the parents typically hang up a clothesline with small presents clipped to it. Partygoers reach up and pull down a little gift as a party favor before leaving. Family birthday celebrations are often lengthy events, covering both lunch and dinner. Piroshkis, which are fried dumplings that can be savory or sweet, are popular birthday treats, as are double-crusted fruit pies with the top crust bearing the name of the birthday boy or girl.

tion at home. Food is a centerpiece of many Russian holidays and celebrations. Big multi-course meals with family are part of many New Year's Day celebrations. New Year's Day is a bigger deal than Christmas, which was given little recognition during the Soviet era. For kids in Russia, the highlight of New Year's Day is Ded Moroz (Grandfather Frost) and his granddaughter Snegurochka (Snow Maiden). They bring presents to children and leave them under the Novogodnaya Yolka, or New Year's tree. Families usually go out after midnight on New Year's Eve to see fireworks and attend other festivities.

Many families in Russia celebrate New Year's Day twice, on January 1 and 14. That is because in the old Julian calendar, the new year began on what is now January 14. The Julian calendar dates back to the time of Julius Caesar; although it is rarely used today, the Russian Orthodox Church still uses it to set holidays. The Orthodox Christmas is celebrated on January 7, and the Christmas celebration continues through January 19. Many families get dressed up and visit friends, while the kids get small gifts from the homes they visit during the Christmas season.

Russian families also mark holidays that are based on the history and politics of the country. For example, there is Defender of the Motherland Day on February 23, which is a way to honor soldiers throughout Russia's history who protected the country from invaders. It is also referred to as Men's Day and is a time when boys and men alike are given special attention and good wishes inside and outside the home. Sometimes they receive presents. Girls and women have their turn to receive gifts and fond recognition on International Women's Day on March 8. While this was originally a day marked by activism and protests for women's rights around the world, it has also become the unofficial start of spring in Russia. Many Russian families also attend parades for Victory Day on May 9. It was originally created to honor soldiers who died during World War II, but it has grown to become a way to recognize veterans of all wars.

Work and school take up a lot of a family's time in Russia, but families still enjoy doing things together, either at home or out in their communities. Whether it is a long dinner filled with stories or a weekend at the dacha in the country, many close-knit Russian families try to make the most of their time together.

CHAPTER THREE

Education and Work

On the first day of a new school year at Moscow's School No. 1582, first-grade students are putting on a skit about sailors looking for the school bell that may have been stolen by pirates. The fun and festivities at this school are similar to first-day activities taking place at schools across the country. Schools in Russia celebrate the start of a new school year with concerts, dancing, skits, and performers such as clowns, acrobats, jugglers, and magicians. "Our goal here is to create all the conditions for children to grow and learn as individuals. We want them to like it, to feel part of it, and that begins from the first hour,"[12] says principal Yevgenia Rybakova.

Celebrating the start of a brand-new school year is a symbol of the importance Russians place on education. Education and literacy have long been a priority. Reading and appreciating Tolstoy and other literary giants has been a rite of passage for young people in Russia for decades. During especially challenging economic times, even poor families maintained the best home libraries they could afford. To own a rare book was to own a real treasure.

Today, whether parents are highly educated professionals or less educated and working in a trade, their children are strongly encouraged to make education the priority in their lives. School meetings to discuss curriculum changes are often packed with concerned parents. Teenagers are discouraged from getting part-time jobs so they can focus on their studies. And even if students must travel long distances to get to school—as is the case in many rural regions in Russia—parents still make sure their kids get an education. In tiny towns such as Kalach and Sankin in southwestern Russia, students take train rides of nearly an hour to get to school.

High Level of Literacy

The Russian Federation holds the distinction of having the highest percentage of adults with a college degree (53.5 percent) of any nation, according to the Organisation for Economic Co-operation and Development. Russia also has one of the world's highest literacy rates; 99 percent of the population is able to read and write by age fifteen. Several factors may be responsible for those numbers. Mandatory schooling starts at age six in Russia, though many children attend preschool programs—many of which are free and sponsored by the government. School is compulsory for kids up to age fifteen—and average class sizes in both primary and secondary schools is under twenty, which is among the smallest in Europe. After age fifteen, students are encouraged to stay in school for another two years to get ready for vocational training or a traditional college education.

The vast majority of Russian students attend public schools, which are overseen at the federal level. Regional authorities can establish some of their own programs as long as they do not conflict with those of the national Ministry of Education and Science. Less than 1 percent of young people in Russia attend a private school. The relatively few private schools in Russia are often geared toward kids who plan to go to college in the United States or somewhere else abroad. A focus on learning English or another language is often at the center of a private school's curriculum.

Children who grow up in farming communities may take long bus rides to attend schools in nearby towns. In more remote regions, the children may attend a boarding school in a distant town and not see their families for months at a time. The Nenets in Siberia send their children off in helicopters dispatched by the Ministry of Education and Science to a federal boarding school for nine months at a time. The school emphasizes Nenets culture with folk art on the walls and small Nenets-style tents in the classrooms to remind the kids of their villages hundreds of miles away.

Primary and Secondary School

In more traditional primary schools in Russia, students from age six to ten are there from 8:30 a.m. to 3:30 p.m. The day usually starts with an announcement from the principal about why studying hard and listening to the teachers are important. Only about three hours

Schools in Russia celebrate the start of a new school year with balloons, dancing, and performers. The celebrations symbolize the importance Russians place on education and literacy.

of each day is spent on academic instruction. Art, music, and recreation, combined with morning snack and lunch, round out the rest of the day. The primary school year is also shorter than in many Western countries: usually 169 days versus 180 days in the United States, for example.

The calendar changes in secondary school. A student's last couple of years of secondary school (similar to eleventh and twelfth grades in the United States) are considerably longer, averaging 210 days a year. That is one of the longest school years of any developed nation. "School is 85 percent and sometimes 90 percent of your life," says Sergey Klementyev, a Russian graduate student who also teaches English in secondary school. "And by school, I mean tons of studying. This experience may vary in cities and towns, but all of my teen students tell me about their school and homework when I ask them about their plans for the weekend or when I just say, 'How are you?'"[13]

The school calendar is similar to that in the United States, including a long summer vacation. Most schools run from Monday through Friday, but some schools offer additional instruction on Saturdays. The classroom environment tends to be formal and disciplined in Russia. Students stand when a teacher enters the room, and they greet their instructor with "Good morning" or "Good afternoon." Many tests are given orally by the teacher, one-on-one with each student.

After school, secondary students can expect at least two or three hours of homework a night. This is in addition to music lessons, sports, and other activities. It does not leave a lot of spare time for Russian teens during the week or any time during the school year, for that matter. "You are rarely expected to work during the school year to support yourself," said Russian college student Dmitry Dobrovolskiy. "You fully rely financially on your parents (in secondary school)."[14]

> "We don't have the same lessons every day. Each day means different subjects, so sometimes your head may explode due to the amount of diverse information you devour."[15]
>
> —Sergey Klementyev, a Russian graduate student and English teacher

Subjects Students Study

Russian high school students usually cannot pick their classes. The secondary school curriculum is the same for all students. It includes Russian language, history, and literature; science; math; and the arts, such as drawing, painting, vocal and instrument instruction, theater, and dance. "But we don't have the same lessons every day," says Klementyev. "Each day means different subjects, so sometimes your head may explode due to the amount of diverse information you devour."[15]

Soviet-era schools made patriotic programs a required part of a child's education, emphasizing service to the motherland and discouraging the negative aspects of Soviet history, such as the oppression of dissidents and limits on freedom and travel. Modern educators wrestle with how to teach these subjects, but they do not shy away from controversial topics. "We now use many different history textbooks, and encourage students to consider alternative interpretations of events. Students are frequently divided into teams to debate controversial issues, rather than being told what to think. This is new,"[16] said primary school teacher Andrei Davidov.

However, Russian schools have not completely abandoned Soviet-style education either. In the old days, schools often included military-style programs in which students wore uniforms, marched, and even learned how to handle firearms. Some of those same activities have returned to Russian schools. One such class teaches students how to safely assemble an AK-47 (Russian assault rifle). "We're not trying to make soldiers

Russian high school students usually cannot pick their classes. The curriculum is the same for all students and includes Russian language, history, literature, science, math, and the arts.

of these children, just good citizens who love their country," says Artur Lutsishin, director of Moscow's School No. 1465. "For the past 15 years or so we have gradually been recovering our understanding that we live in a great country. Not the country that lost the cold war, but one that's equal to the others. It's only good that our state is paying closer attention to patriotic education."[17]

Despite this recent emphasis on military training and political history, plenty of Russian students would rather focus on the basics of science, math, literature, and less-controversial subjects. "I'm not very political, and we don't talk about this stuff in class much," says Artyem Chinkov, an eleventh-grade student who wants a career in the petroleum industry. "I think values mainly come from the family, from the community. I come to school to study."[18]

University Education

More than half of Russia's young people go on to attend college. Those who wish to go to college spend two extra years in secondary school taking college prep classes. These classes help get them ready for college entrance exams. Russia's Unified State Exam is similar in many ways to the SAT. It takes from three to four hours and tests reading and math skills. Some students also take exams in other subjects, such as foreign languages and various sciences. There is a lot of competition to get into Russia's top universities, including Lomonosov Moscow State University and Novosibirsk State University. So university-bound students tend to take their studies and their entrance exams very seriously. Most students who want to go to college are accepted, though they may not get into their first choice of schools.

The typical course of study is four years for a bachelor's degree and two more years for a master's degree. Students do pay for this education, but tuition at most universities costs less than $2,000 per year—and in some instances it costs nothing at all.

Living expenses are the responsibility of the student or the student's family, however.

In Russia university students are truly held accountable to their parents, peers, and themselves. A student's exam grades may be read in front of the entire class or posted next to the student's name on the professor's door. Parents often get a letter from a professor if a student is not doing well. In many classes a final exam is worth 90 percent to 100 percent of the grade. Classes are predetermined for each major. There are no academic advisors because there is little choice about which classes to take.

Some universities focus on subjects such as engineering or business, but many offer a broad range of majors. Russia's highest-ranked university is Lomonosov Moscow State University, which has about 7,000 undergraduate students, more than 40,000 graduate and postgraduate students, 380 departments, 15 research institutes, and 6 branch campuses. Another of Russia's best universities is Novosibirsk State University. Though small, with only about 6,000 students, the school appeals to many young people because it is located in the thriving nightlife section of Novosibirsk, Russia's third-largest city. Saint Petersburg State University, which has more than 32,000 undergraduate and graduate students, is Russia's oldest university. It also draws thousands of foreign students to its sprawling campus every year. Students fascinated with science, technology, engineering, and math (STEM) subjects find opportunities at the Moscow Institute of Physics and Technology, which has about 5,000 students and encourages research in the real world, not just within the university.

Vocational Education

Many young people in Russia enroll in vocational institutes rather than universities. These institutes, sometimes referred to as colleges or professional schools, are higher education programs that provide intensive training in a trade that will lead directly to a job after graduation. A little less than half of the students who leave secondary school, or about 1.5 million young people, attend vocational institutes. There are nearly four thousand such schools in Russia, most of which are public—and most do not require any type of admissions test.

Ballet Schools and Russia's Most Graceful Students

The Bolshoi Ballet Academy may be the most famous Russian dance school, but it is only one of several prestigious ballet programs in the country. A few years after the Bolshoi Ballet Academy was formed in Moscow in 1773, the Vaganova Academy of Russian Ballet was created in Saint Petersburg. Since then, ballet schools large and small have cropped up in Russia's cities, drawing thousands of boys and girls to learn the discipline and artistic expression of this international dance.

Competition for admission to ballet schools is stiff—especially for girls. Dozens, and sometimes hundreds, of girls might seek one available place at one of the more prestigious ballet schools. The entrance examination and audition look at children's health, build, flexibility, coordination, and posture, as well their musicality and dance skills. The ballet academies accept children starting at ages eight to ten and provide eight years of schooling and ballet training. Once accepted to a ballet academy, a student must continue to take a full load of regular school classes while spending hours a day rehearsing. The ultimate goal is to obtain a position with a top ballet company. Those who do not may be hired by lower-tier dance troupes or join foreign ballet companies. Russian ballet dancers are in high demand in international troupes, as the achievement of surviving the demands of a Russian ballet academy is well known in the dance world.

Many of the schools have relationships with local governments or private industry to prepare students for specific jobs in a particular field. In a region where mining is common, for instance, a vocational institute might focus on training students for mining careers. Schools with strong programs in metallurgy (the practice of taking raw metal ores, such as iron, and converting them into useful products, such as steel) are usually located near industrial areas. Other areas of study include aquaculture, marine navigation, machinery, computer programming, and medical technology.

Some vocational schools are very small. The Arctic College of the Peoples of the North, for instance, has 125 students and has programs in mining and agriculture, but it also helps train students to become reindeer herders, cooks, and mechanics. It is located in the remote Sakha region of northeastern Russia. And because it caters to the indigenous peoples of the area, the school also teaches students about the history and traditions of their culture. Larger vocational schools include the Syktyvkar Forest Institute in a scenic area of northwestern Russia. Forestry-related programs cover engineering, woodlands management, wood processing, and some computer technologies. The school has about 4,900 students and has programs affiliated with other European forestry schools.

Military Service

Regardless of whether they attend a vocational school or a university, most young men in Russia spend at least one year serving in the military. This service must be done between ages eighteen and twenty-seven. Many young men get their military service out of the way before beginning vocational or university education. Fulfilling their military requirements early can help young men get into college because in some instances, military service can take the place of entrance exams. Others delay their military obligation until after completing their education.

Although military service is mandatory, not everyone serves. Those who stay in school long enough to earn a PhD often surpass the age twenty-seven requirement. Young men may also work in jobs as police officers or firefighters to fulfill their military service obligation. Also, being the father of a young child can exempt a young man from service.

However, some young men see the military as their best—and sometimes only—means of earning a living. This is especially true in Russia's many small towns and villages. "Unemployment is quite high in the [rural] regions, so young men agree to serve. By contrast, very few residents of Moscow or St. Petersburg would fancy joining the army,"[19] says military expert Vladimir Dvorkin.

Job Prospects for Russian Youth

Although Russia's unemployment rate fell to 6 percent in 2016, job prospects in rural areas are slim. Many young people growing up in Russia's small towns and villages are moving to the cities in hopes of finding well-paying jobs. "Once out of secondary school, two thirds of young people leave their provincial communities for regional centers never to come back,"[20] says Russian sociologist Ilya Kashnitsky.

Young adults are more likely to find jobs in the cities—or in regions with strong ties to industry. Companies that do business internationally offer good career prospects, especially for those who are fluent in English. Government jobs and positions in technology, manufacturing, and sales are among the other sought-after careers. "Jobs in engineering and industry will see a good growth in Russia,"[21] says career headhunter Alena Vladimirskaya, curator of the Career Guidance cluster at the 2016 Moscow International Education Fair. Since Russia is a world leader in oil and gas production, for instance, a wide range of career options, from drillers to geologists to energy company executives and salespeople, is available. Machine manufacturing is also a major industry, mostly centered in Moscow, Saint Petersburg, and the industrial cities in the Ural Mountain region and western Siberia. The chemical, mining, and metallurgic industries are also major draws for job seekers.

Seeing a need to prepare students for careers in these and other fields, some universities are adding more on-the-job training and internships. Some private companies are even setting up their own departments at universities to provide very job-specific training to students so that students are ready to start work when they graduate.

No Guarantee of Prosperity

A university degree does not automatically lead to a job, let alone a great career. As many as two-thirds of university graduates cannot find work in Russia right after graduation. Many of them take up to six months to find a job. And while many people in Russia (and in much of Europe) work with a contract with their employer, about one in four young Russians work without a contract and without any long-term employment confidence. And even if a university graduate lands a decent job, he or she may still struggle to pay the bills. Tatiana Golubeva says:

> Becoming a doctor is highly prestigious and a very well-paid profession in the U.S. But in Russia, most doctors are struggling to meet ends. The State healthcare is still

free or almost free for people, and funding by the government does not provide for high salaries. Of course, doctors who work at private clinics make better money—especially dentists and plastic surgeons—but for the majority of the population, these services are too expensive. Most teachers and scientists also have low salaries. But people who work in businesses, especially international companies that require fluent English are making good money. Recently, working in government organizations has also become popular, as salaries there have substantially increased.[22]

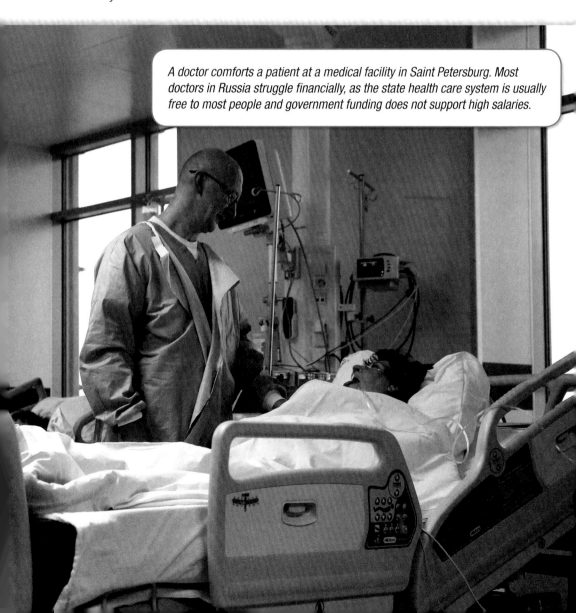

A doctor comforts a patient at a medical facility in Saint Petersburg. Most doctors in Russia struggle financially, as the state health care system is usually free to most people and government funding does not support high salaries.

More young women in Russia are also pursuing careers beyond the typical role of secretary or teacher. Women's employment in Russia is among the highest in the world. Russian women are not being held back by older societal expectations of women. "I think that people who are now 20 to 30 years old are quite progressive in terms of gender equality, and that girls are making a career for themselves and have strong ideas of what they want to do,"[23] Gołubeva says. Vladimirskaya founded one of Russia's largest online recruiting companies. She says that it is important to be her own boss. "I wanted to make my own story, not play a part in someone else's story,"[24] she says.

The Things That Matter
Many teenagers and young adults in today's Russia have experienced financial difficulties—either on their own or through the

Making the Military a Career

About 1.3 million men and women serve in the armed forces of the Russian Federation. Most of them are men (called conscripts) serving their required year of service, but an increasing number are women who choose to join the military or men who decide to make a career in uniform after their military obligations have been met.

Only about 10 percent of Russian military personnel are women. They include enlisted soldiers and sailors, as well as officers. The Ministry of Defense is developing programs to retain men for long-term military careers and to encourage more women to join. The ministry is doing this by improving the contracts men and women sign when they volunteer for military careers. About a quarter of those serving in the armed forces are under contract. "Those who serve under contract love it in the army," says Valentina Melnikova, executive secretary of the Committee of Soldiers' Mothers, a group that advocates for better conditions for people in the military—especially the conscripts. "They are paid well and entitled to days off. As for conscripts, the situation is quite different." Conscripts get lower pay and have little say in where they are deployed. Soldiers who enlist under contracts have more choice about the branch of the military in which they serve.

Quoted in Marina Obrazkova, "More Russians Find Military Service Appealing," Russia Beyond the Headlines, March 12, 2014. www.rbth.com.

experiences of their families. For these young people, youthful dreams of unlimited wealth and luxury have been replaced by hopes for stability and economic well-being. "They want to travel, but their salaries are in rubles, the value of which has been halved by the economic crisis," writes *National Geographic* reporter Julia Ioffe. "Some want to open their own businesses but don't know how to scale the dangerous slopes of local corruption. So they train their sights lower. They want a house or apartment, a car, and a family."[25]

Alexander Kuznetsov's story reflects this reality. Kuznetsov, now twenty, grew up in Nizhniy Tagil in eastern Russia. His father left the family when Alexander was just a toddler. The family struggled. "For me," he says, "the most important thing is family." He wants to serve in the military, and he hopes his military service will help him get a well-paying job as a police officer or in the country's federal security agency. This—and family—are what matter most to him right now. He says, "I really want to have a stable income."[26]

CHAPTER FOUR

Social Life

A small group of teens gather at a Starbucks on a Saturday afternoon, sipping frothy sweetened coffee drinks and texting more friends to meet them for a movie later. It could be a scene played out in Seattle, Washington, or Sarasota, Florida, or any of a thousand other cities around the world. In this case the kids are Russian, and it is a typical weekend night for them in Kotelniki, a suburb of Moscow. They are getting ready to see the latest *Star Wars* movie in the IMAX theater at the Mega Belaya Dacha, a shiny new shopping mall. "Russian kids have so many of the same preferences as Americans that really very little separates them," S. Elliott Estebo says. "As in America, everyone growing up in Russia now knows 'The Simpsons,' or 'Simpsoniy' in Russian, and they've listened to Drake and Rihanna and want, if they don't already have, the newest iPhone and Xbox."[27]

As in any other country, the social lives and leisurely pursuits of young people in Russia are influenced first by family and second by the communities in which they live. In cities such as Moscow and Saint Petersburg, more jobs and more money translate to more things to do. But in the small towns and villages mostly in eastern Russia, many factories and other businesses have closed and people struggle to get by. These towns are less likely to have the social and cultural amenities found in the big cities.

Socializing in the City

For most teenagers, getting around in cities like Moscow and Saint Petersburg usually means walking or taking public transportation. Public transportation in these cities is the number one method of travel. It is cheap and convenient, and it runs all day and most of the night. Private cars are a less common form of getting around the cities, especially for youth, who cannot even get a driver's license until age eighteen. And once they have a license, they are unlikely to have a car.

But that does not seem to stop young people from meeting up with their friends. Weeknights are mostly reserved for schoolwork, but weekends are when teens flee the home to explore the city with friends. A typical weekend night could include hanging out and sipping thick and delicious hot chocolate at GUM, Moscow's century-old shopping mall with a dazzling glass roof, or dancing late into the night at any of dozens of clubs scattered throughout Russia's largest city. The age to get into clubs that serve alcohol is officially eighteen in Russia, but plenty of teens know where they can go if they are underage. Young people are especially drawn to places with specific themes, like Ping Pong Club Moscow, which is where young people hang out, drink tea, and play Ping-Pong in a hipster-inspired basement club. The massive five-story B2 is a club that features live concerts on multiple floors, a 1970s- and 1980s-themed disco on another floor, and a restaurant that includes outdoor seating in the summer.

> "Everyone growing up in Russia now knows 'The Simpsons,' or 'Simpsoniy' in Russian, and they've listened to Drake and Rihanna and want, if they don't already have, the newest iPhone and Xbox."[27]
>
> —S. Elliott Estebo, an American who taught English in Russia

On weekends young people also roam Saint Petersburg's downtown area, which is home to one of Russia's most thriving music scenes. Young music fans fill the city's many music clubs and concert halls throughout the year. In summer though, Saint Petersburg really shines. During the white nights phenomenon across all of northern Russia, when daylight lasts long into the night, plenty of romantic young Russian couples stroll along the city's riverbanks in the hazy midnight glow of a seemingly endless summer day. "It's a magical city, like no other place in Russia," says Irina Nabok, a student in Saint Petersburg. "Especially now, during White Nights. It becomes the city of love."[28]

Russia has also experienced an explosion in its hip-hop scene. Freestyle rap can be heard from kids on street corners in Moscow, while girls and boys who love to dance rehearse for hip-hop dance competitions that are springing up around the country. In

Young people hang out and eat snacks at a park in Saint Petersburg. Most Russian teens spend all of their free time on weekends with their friends.

2016 a group of tween Russian boys and girls took second place in the World Hip Hop Dance Championships in Las Vegas, Nevada.

Socializing in Russia can also mean hanging out with friends in cafés, city parks, video game arcades, and at the movies. Groups of friends can often be seen simply roaming the streets, content to be together or on the lookout for something to do. Spending time with friends gives kids a little time away from their parents and other family members. Because so many Russian families live in small apartments, teens highly value a little family-free time. Many parents allow their teens to be out without having to check in or announce where they are going or with whom.

Curfews

Wandering around the cities is not altogether safe. Crime is an ongoing problem, as is youth drinking and drug use. One way Russian authorities have sought to help kids stay safe, reduce juvenile crime, and avoid drugs and alcohol is by instituting a curfew. In many urban areas of Russia, including Moscow and Saint Petersburg, a government-imposed curfew means unaccompanied youths must be off the streets between 10:00 p.m. and 6:00 a.m. The curfew first went into effect in 2009, with government officials saying it was meant to protect young people from street violence.

Not all teens appreciate the government's efforts. Katya, a seventeen-year-old in Moscow, says that the curfew laws tend to backfire, challenging kids to flout authority. She explains:

> They are talking about stopping teenagers from taking drugs, smoking and drinking, but the funny thing is that the more you limit people, the more they want to do forbidden things. Sitting outside laughing is much better than spending nights hanging around in stuffy doorways irritating old ladies. Most of us just think it's another useless effort that shows the government's inability to stop crime. People who get into trouble will find a way to do so anyway.[29]

"They are talking about stopping teenagers from taking drugs, smoking and drinking, but the funny thing is that the more you limit people, the more they want to do forbidden things."[29]

—Katya, a seventeen-year-old in Moscow, on government curfew laws

Small Town Social Life

Crime and curfews are less of a concern in Russia's small towns, but opportunities for weekend fun are also less plentiful. Even so, young people growing up outside of the major cities find ways to enjoy an active social life. School dances, plays, and concerts take on a greater role in small towns than they do in larger cities. With fewer clubs, malls, arcades, cafés, and other hangouts, small-town kids have to be more resourceful when it comes to generating fun.

In some rural areas outdoor activities are popular with youth. Since the Winter Olympics were held in Sochi, Russia, in 2014, snowboarding has taken off as a new favorite recreational pursuit of teens across the country. Best friends Vlad and Sasha, both fifteen, use a snow-covered hill in the middle of their Siberian hometown, Khanty-Mansiysk, to practice snowboarding. The hill is a short distance from the beautiful Cathedral of the Resurrection of Christ. "There are two ski resorts in Khanty-Mansiysk, so there's no need to go far away if you want to ski or snowboard," says Sasha. "But this hill is even closer so we come here. No one in the church minds that we snowboard here."[30]

An Olympian snowboards at the 2014 Winter Olympics held in Sochi, Russia. Since then, snowboarding has taken off as a new recreational pursuit for youth across the country.

Kids who do not find healthy outlets for socializing and recreation sometimes turn to alcohol or drugs to alleviate their boredom. Even though the legal drinking age in Russia is eighteen, the law is inconsistently enforced. That means younger teens often have little difficulty getting their hands on alcohol. "The problem is that kids start drinking around 14–15 years of age regularly," said Evgeny Bryun, the Russian Federation Ministry of Health's chief narcologist. (Narcology, a term used in Russia, refers to the study of alcohol and drug abuse.) "Dependency takes a few years to form, so when they're brought to us, the process has already been formed, and we cannot always pull them out of this tough situation."[31] Teen drinking is not a problem only in rural areas, but it tends to be more widespread in these areas, where there are fewer possibilities for socializing.

Sex and Dating

Research suggests that Russia's relatively high teen pregnancy rate is largely related to the consumption of alcohol by underage youths. After a steady increase in the teen pregnancy rate in Russia through the early 2000s, the rate is starting to fall, according to the World Bank. However, at twenty-three per one thousand women age fifteen to nineteen, the teen pregnancy rate is still among the highest among developed nations. There are also relatively few services available to provide family planning information to young people or assistance to girls who become pregnant. "I felt so lonely, and there was no one whom I could ask for help,"[32] says Nadya, a Russian orphan who became pregnant at sixteen. She soon found a nurturing mentor in a group called Kidsave Russia. But a lack of information about sex and pregnancy for young people in all walks of life in Russia remains a problem.

Russian youths do not receive sex education in school. A survey conducted by the Russian Federal State Statistics Service and the Ministry of Health, and funded by the United Nations Population Fund, found that about 85 percent of students want more information on sexually transmitted diseases. About 70 percent of teen girls in the survey said they wanted more information to help protect against unwanted pregnancies and sexually transmitted diseases.

Russian youths are usually given a lot of independence by their parents, which can lead to experimentation with sex, alcohol, and drugs. Russian youths, in general, have a fairly casual attitude about sex and dating. However, teens who have strong religious views, such as those preached in the Russian Orthodox Church, are more conservative. There are other fairly conservative aspects of teen dating in Russia, too. Dating does not usually begin until age sixteen or seventeen, and boys are often expected to pay, though plenty of kids share the cost of dates. Group dates are also very common throughout Russia, with couples and their friends gathering at dances, clubs, or weekend music and arts festivals.

LGBT Youths in Russia

Dating and socializing in general are more complicated and even dangerous for LGBT youth in Russia. Russian society as a whole is not accepting of homosexuality. A 2013 law, for example, banned the dissemination of any materials that present homosexuality as normal or natural. Violence and increasing antigay sentiments have also become a problem for LGBT youth. As Ty Cobb, global engagement director of the Human Rights Campaign Foundation, explains, "The evidence is clear. State-sponsored homophobia and transphobia in Russia poses a direct threat to the safety and welfare of LGBT Russians, and that threat is growing."[33]

An organization called Deti-404 was formed originally as an online community where LGBT youths could find support. Volunteers traveled around Russia counseling young people and giving them strategies for dealing with unsupportive relatives and bullying in school and elsewhere. However, Russia does not openly support nontraditional relationships or efforts to assist gays or increase awareness among the general public. Deti-404 was shut down by the government in the fall of 2016 for disseminating banned information. Its loss created a void for LBGT youths, but other social media outlets are widely used by all kinds of young people in Russia to connect to others with common interests.

Anna Grigoryeva, a Moscow native and college student, is also an LGBT activist. She says the LGBT community is Russia is filled with "amazing, strong people," which is necessary in the fight against antigay laws and harassment. She notes that public protests and increased awareness (both inside and outside Russia)

Parkour Makes a Leap in Popularity

Parkour is an activity that borrows from military obstacle course training. Practitioners try to get from one location to another as fast as possible by running, climbing, jumping, vaulting, and doing whatever other moves are necessary to get past obstacles such as walls, stairways, fences, benches, and other items in an urban terrain. It is become a wildly popular sport in Russia, with exceptional traceurs (parkour practitioners) posting videos of their exploits online. It has also become deadly in a few rare cases, as young people have died trying to make dangerous leaps from great heights.

Efforts to teach parkour safety are under way through a variety of outlets. In 2010 the Parkour Academy was established in Moscow. The Russian Orthodox Church also sponsors a parkour center for teenagers on probation to help teach them discipline and to give them a healthy way to spend their time. Famous Russian parkour artist Evgeny Krynin teaches the kids about life and his acrobatic pastime. "Many of them have been thrown out of school. As a result they have few aspirations and a great deal of anger inside them. But you have to be calm and concentrated to perfect a difficult movement," Krynin says. "It teaches them that every obstacle can be overcome with enough perseverance."

Quoted in Lucy Ash, "Why Russia's Orthodox Church Is Teaching Teenagers Parkour," BBC, October 17, 2012. www.bbc.com.

are creating support for Russia's LGBT community. "All of a sudden the Russian liberal establishment is a lot more aware of LGBT issues and that's an unexpected effect of all of this,"[34] she says.

Social Media and Gaming

Like teenagers around the world, Russian youths also share the tendency to document their lives online with apps such as Instagram and Snapchat. Facebook is not used much in Russia, however. Instead, one of the most popular social media sites is VKontakte (VK), which is similar to Facebook and is used by millions of Russian teens. They use it to send public and private messages, engage in group chats, play browser-based games, and share videos, music, and other content.

Internet access is available in most parts of Russia, even in some remote parts of eastern and northern Siberia, but government censorship of VK content or other websites is common. If a music video, for example, is considered lewd and inappropriate for younger eyes, it will be banned. But resourceful Russian teens can get around online censorship fairly easily. A browser plug-in called Hola can make it look as though they are browsing from a country other than Russia. A lesser-known browser called Opera Turbo also lets Russian youths go online censor-free because it goes through servers in Norway, which has far greater Internet freedom than Russia.

Video gaming in Russia has grown rapidly in recent years, and now the country is one of the biggest video game markets in the world. Russian kids might gather at a friend's house or at an arcade for hours of casual and highly competitive gaming. Known as eSports, competitive video gaming now gets financial support from the Russian government in the same way as soccer and

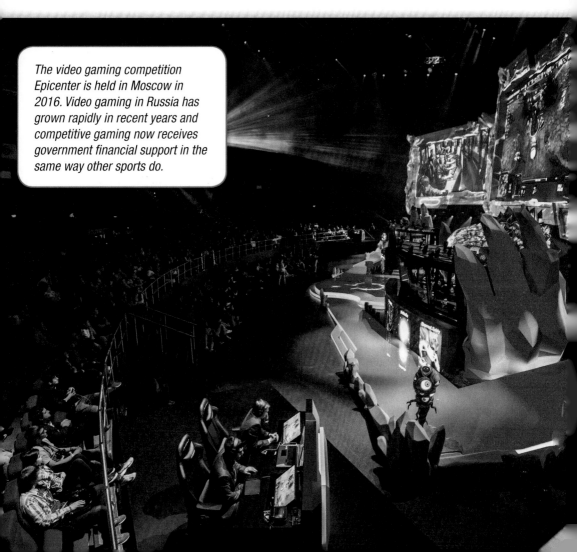

The video gaming competition Epicenter is held in Moscow in 2016. Video gaming in Russia has grown rapidly in recent years and competitive gaming now receives government financial support in the same way other sports do.

other sports do. Russian champions in eSports can now claim titles such as Master of Sports of Russia, International Master of Sports, and Honored Master of Sports.

Togetherness Through Religion

Though technology is transforming the way Russian kids communicate and spend their time, many young people form friendships in something very old: the church.

The Russian Orthodox Church, by far the largest religious group in the country, is involved in several programs aimed at reaching more young people. As the church has grown in its outreach since the Soviet days, when it was essentially outlawed, the number of youth groups has been rising.

But the church is doing much more than simply organizing youth groups at the local parish. One initiative, Orthodoxy and Sport, promotes a physically and spiritually healthy lifestyle. As part of this effort, young people around the country are invited to gatherings known as Sorochinsky meetings. These started in 2014. They are gatherings of prominent members of the clergy, along with well-known scholars, athletes, artists, and other cultural figures. The public figures share their stories of faith to help inspire the young people in attendance. Organizers of a Russian youth Christian movement called Sorok Sorokov ("forty times forty") want to dispel the image of the Russian Orthodox Church as a place just for "the grandmas in headscarves and the exalted part of society,"[35] according to a reporter for the Russia Insider website. To achieve this goal, the group has also organized volunteer programs that help orphans and the homeless—and young people have responded to these efforts by getting involved.

The Sporting Life

Whether they live in big cities or small towns, many Russian teens find a healthy social outlet in sports. Russian high schools do not have their own sports teams. Instead, local sports teams are run by community arts and recreation centers. These centers, known as Houses of Culture, usually include a gymnasium and other recreational facilities, an auditorium for the performing arts, and space for community meetings, classes, and other programs.

Afisha Picnic

Summer music festivals are nearly as common as borscht in Russia, but one festival in particular is geared toward teens, especially those with a wide range of interests beyond music. Afisha Picnic is a staple of summer in Moscow. The one-day music festival features Russian bands and pop stars, as well as musicians from around the world, on several stages. But every year the nonmusic offerings are often just as interesting and well attended. In recent years Afisha Picnic's lineups have included karting and radio-controlled cars, poetry readings, an open-air film festival, classes on graffiti, Thai massage, squirt gun games, pottery and glassblowing classes, lectures, roller disco, yoga classes, fashion shows, and lots of gastronomic delights. Organizers of Afisha Picnic enforce a strict no-alcohol policy to ensure attendance by teenagers and even families with younger kids. The festival started in 2004 and is held every year in an area about 6 miles (9.7 km) southeast of Moscow called Kolomenskoye, which belonged to one of the czars more than one hundred years ago. The land is now a nature preserve that includes a historical museum. But for one day every summer, it is the site of a truly memorable picnic.

Summer sports draw many young people. Soccer is the most popular team sport in Russia, with youth leagues drawing kids as young as four. Tennis has also become more popular for young people in recent years, especially with the success of athletes such as Russia native Maria Sharapova—winner of several major international tournaments.

Russian kids also participate in a variety of winter sports. Ice hockey is one of the most popular winter sports in Russia. Boys and girls alike play on youth teams across the country. Moscow alone has about thirty youth hockey leagues. Talented players can sign professional contracts at age sixteen, though a few turn pro as young as thirteen. Many of the nation's top hockey players have even gone on to play in North America's National Hockey League. Other popular winter sports include figure skating, speed skating, and bobsledding.

Appreciation of the Arts

While sports are a popular pursuit of many Russian youths, so too are the arts. Common interests in music draw together kids of all ages. Music festivals for all genres of music take place throughout the year and in many locations—although most are in western Russia. Young people hitchhike, take the train, or find some other way to get to the festival sites and camp out for the duration. A three-day summer electronic music festival, called Alfa Future People and held along the Volga River, drew forty thousand people in 2015. For young fans of British rock and pop music, the annual Ahmad Tea Music Festival in Moscow is a big draw. The festival's slogan is "There Is No Life Without Tea and Music."

On a more serene note, some Russian young people find their musical roots in the sanctuaries of their local Russian Orthodox churches. The Children's Choir of Russia, formed in 2013 with the support of the church and the Russian Ministry of Culture, drew thousands of kids ages nine to fifteen from all of Russia's eighty-three regions to auditions. The thousand-voice choir performed in concert halls around the country and was part of the beautiful closing ceremonies at the 2014 Sochi Winter Olympics.

> "Friends are very important for Russian people, and best friends are the ones you know from childhood."[36]
>
> —Tatiana Golubeva, a Moscow native and blogger

Like young people worldwide, Russian youth might take part in any number of activities for fun, but they are often happy just hanging out with their friends and doing nothing much at all. "Friends are very important for Russian people, and best friends are the ones you know from childhood," Tatiana Golubeva says. "My best friend is a girl I met at the age of 7. We went to elementary school together and we still talk every day."[36]

CHAPTER FIVE

Hopes and Challenges

In today's Russia young people are surrounded by the promise of an exciting future spurred on by rapidly advancing technology and ever-expanding educational opportunities. But economic troubles in many parts of the country, an often oppressive government, religious strife, and changing moral values are conspiring to make young people there more anxious about the future. Facing an uncertain future, young Russians seem split between those who see their country heading down a troubling path and others who are more optimistic and confident in Russia's ability to endure.

According to a recent study by the independent nonprofit global think tank IRFI, many Russian young people are dissatisfied with the policies of their government and would like to see change in their country. A survey that appears in that study, called "Russia: Youth and Politics," shows the areas of most concern for young Russians are government corruption and poverty. However, the study author concludes, most youth are unwilling to actively seek changes in these and other areas of dissatisfaction. In fact, a 2016 article in *National Geographic* states that 83 percent of Russians age eighteen to twenty-four say they have not participated in any kind of political or civil society activity. And yet some of Russia's young people are expressing their views by joining political movements.

Nationalist Movements Attracting Youth

Young Russians have been joining nationalist groups in rapidly increasing numbers, according to Stratfor Worldview, an international political research organization. Stratfor noted that, for example, the youth nationalist organization Nashi grew from about 170,000 members in 2007 to more than 600,000 by the end of 2011. Nationalist movements in Russia mean different things to different people. Some nationalist groups hope for a future in which the territories that once made up the Soviet Union come together again to form a bigger, stronger Russia. The groups within this movement are driven by frustration that Russia has seemingly slipped from its place as a world superpower. Other nationalist groups believe that Russia should be for Russians only, meaning people of Slavic descent. They oppose immigration and want to limit the rights and opportunities of people of different ethnicities and national origins. Regardless of their main political or social priorities, young nationalists see themselves as trying to take their country back from various entities that they believe have stolen it from them.

One of the more popular nationalist groups attracting Russian youth is called Set. Set is a youth organization that formed to support Russian president Vladimir Putin's policies and programs. Its leaders have also tried to discourage efforts among other young people to form any organized resistance to those policies. Set, which started with about one thousand members in 2014 and has grown steadily since then, uses social media to attract new members. It promotes itself through speeches, film festivals, and art shows. Set's goal, unlike that of some other youth nationalist groups, is not to bully others into its way of thinking but to promote Russian values and ideas. The group has created pro-Russian patriotic textbooks for kids, for example, and has members who are successful entrepreneurs in their twenties working with the Kremlin on pro-Russian business policies.

Another group, a controversial youth organization called Yunarmiya (Young Army), employs an army-style training and appearance, with red or khaki uniform shirts and berets. Detractors argue that the kids in the program are being brainwashed with heavy-handed pro-Russia propaganda and are being taught to use military-style weapons at an inappropriately young age, possibly endangering their lives. "Attempts to militarize children are a violation of their rights,"[37] says Valentina Melnikova, an advocate for soldiers' rights in Russia. Melnikova and other critics of Yunarmiya and other youth groups that include marching and weapons training in their programs say the groups are part of a broader

Russian youth march in a patriotic rally organized by the nationalist pro-Kremlin youth group Nashi. Young people have been joining nationalist groups in rapidly increasing numbers.

effort by the government to turn back the clock and make Russia a more militaristic society.

Yunarmiya organizers, however, say the goal simply is to encourage young people to embrace Russia's history and its heroes, as well as prepare them to be loyal, productive citizens. The young Yunarmiya members make a pledge when joining: "I swear to aim for victories in studies and sports, to live a healthy lifestyle, to make myself prepared for the service and labour for the sake of the Motherland, to cherish the memory of the heroes who fought for freedom and independence of our Motherland, to be a patriot and a dignified citizen of Russia."[38]

Young Russians Protest Government Corruption

Nationalist movements are not the only ones attracting young Russians. Many young people, especially those in the cities but even those in some other regions of the country, say they are disgusted by reports of widespread corruption in government. They believe these actions threaten both their own futures and the future of their country. "I actually don't like the real situation in Russia now," says Daniel, a student at Moscow State University. "Some things are really disappointing to me, like corruption. It's terrible, but I hope it will all change."[39]

Protests against corruption erupted in early 2017, with thousands of teenagers taking part in demonstrations in eighty-two cities—from Moscow and Saint Petersburg to Siberia and the Far East. At one Moscow demonstration in March 2017, a group of fourteen- and fifteen-year-old girls and boys shouted a chant that was directed at Putin and Prime Minister Dmitry Medvedev. The youths said, "While you were stealing our money, we were growing!"[40]

Svetlana, a seventeen-year-old student who participated in the March demonstration in Saint Petersburg, understands that change will take time in Russia. Nevertheless, she feels it is important for Russians, and especially young people, to speak out. "I realize that a few demonstrations will not change much, but the authorities will understand that people are not satisfied with the results of their work,"[41] she says.

Whether today's young Russians are pro-government or anti-government or somewhere in between, it is clear that uncertainty about the future is stirring up some anxiety. "Well, I hope for a bright future, but who knows what's going to happen next," says Alexey, a Moscow State University student. "It's possible things will turn out not the way we wanted them. There might be war or something. There's a possibility there might be a Third World War."[42]

> "I actually don't like the real situation in Russia now. Some things are really disappointing to me, like corruption. It's terrible, but I hope it will all change."[39]
>
> —Daniel, a student at Moscow State University

Troubled Teens

While most young Russians hope for a brighter future, hopelessness is an all-too-common challenge for many Russian teens. The teen suicide rate in Russia is one of the highest of any nation on earth. In 2017 federal and local authorities investigated a rash of more than one hundred teen suicides that may have been linked to an online game that bullied teens and encouraged them to kill themselves. But experts believe that teen suicide in Russia is a multilayered problem that goes beyond online bullying. It is more likely a reflection of economic, family, political, and social challenges facing the nation's young people. "There's clearly something going on in Russian-speaking countries that creates anxiety and unhappiness. You don't just commit suicide, it's a pretty big decision to make,"[43] says Matthijs Muijen, mental health program manager at the World Health Organization's Regional Office for Europe.

Computer use in general, and greater isolation and loneliness, may be driving Russian youths to the edge. "Kids used to spend more time at school, participating in different after-school activities," says Yelena Shumakova, a supervisor at Your Territory Online, a foundation that provides anonymous online consultations to teenagers in trouble. "There used to be a lot of free workshops and studios and classes, and children had more friends and more mentors they could talk to. Now they spend most of their time alone with their computers."[44]

> "There used to be a lot of free workshops and studios and classes, and children had more friends and more mentors they could talk to. Now they spend most of their time alone with their computers."[44]
>
> —Yelena Shumakova, a supervisor at Your Territory Online, a resource for troubled teens

Computers and online mental health support programs might actually be part of the solution for some troubled young people. In Russia's many remote towns and villages, there are few resources for depression screenings and other mental health services. The situation is a little better in the cities, but in a country that oppresses people for their sexual orientation and limits freedom of expression, there needs to be more outreach to kids in hopes of preventing problems later on, says Evgeny Lyubov, head of the suicide department of the Moscow Scientific Institute of Psychiatry. "School children undergo medical examinations every year—why not throw in screening questions to establish depression? Especially for children aged 14–16—they are at a higher risk,"[45] says Lyubov.

Homelessness

Another daunting problem is youth homelessness, which affects both urban and rural kids. Between 1 million and 5 million Russian youths age seventeen and under are estimated to be homeless. Experts say that youth homelessness is largely the result of dysfunctional families. Parental alcohol abuse is among the chief causes, as is domestic violence, according to a report from the Institute of Modern Russia. The report placed much of the blame on political leaders who have cut education spending and have

Two homeless boys sleep in the basement of an abandoned municipal building in Saint Petersburg. Between 1 and 5 million youth are estimated to be homeless in Russia.

not made it a priority to address the causes and consequences of youth homelessness. The report concludes:

> In today's Russia, this problem serves as the reminder of the crisis in values in the state as a whole, as both the government and the public cynically ignore the outward signs of this serious issue. . . . Russian politicians should consider the fact that youth homelessness is a time bomb: if it is not neutralized, sooner or later, it will explode, and no one dare predict the consequences of the social catastrophe that will follow.[46]

A growing number of charities are working with social service agencies throughout Russia to help take in homeless children and families, as well as improve the quality of orphanages. Their efforts include working with local police and courts to reroute homeless youths who are arrested for drug offenses away from jail and into programs that can house them and help them deal with any drug or alcohol abuse issues.

Era of Opportunity

Despite challenges such as teen suicide and youth homelessness, young Russians have reasons to be optimistic, too. At no other time in Russia's history have there been so many opportunities for smart, ambitious, and hardworking young people. During the Soviet era, the state controlled old and new businesses. Creating and owning a business was not really possible. Now entrepreneurship is drawing young Russians, even in their teens.

Already a successful entrepreneur in the tech field in his early teens, at age seventeen Denis Shelestov launched a company called Shelest Ventures. Its goal is to invest in companies and ideas created by young people for young people. Some early investments include LaxMed, a medical services app, and Tatarcha, an app to help people learn and study the Tatar language. "School entrepreneurship has many advantages," Shelestov says. "Pupils are free of bias and usually have no negative experiences holding them back. When they are taken seriously, they can invent wonders. The best thing is when pupils create for their peers."[47]

And Shelestov is not the only young entrepreneur making the most of his talents and vision. Since the early 2000s Russia has seen an explosion of new business start-ups created by young men and women. Tech business owner and writer Mikhail Naumov says the combination of investors looking for the next big thing in technology, relatively little competition in the Russian tech field, and the support of the government makes this era an "entrepreneurial renaissance." Naumov adds that young Russians have no memory of how difficult it was to get things done in business during the Soviet era. Kids today have reasons to believe that they can be successful. "The abundance of resources, access to information and global markets, institutional support and a rapidly developing startup culture create a perfect storm for entrepreneurial innovation in Russia for the next decade,"[48] says Naumov.

Education Gets a Boost

But there are more reasons to be hopeful about the future in Russia than striking it rich with a tech start-up. Russia is also investing in its universities, which have traditionally not ranked very high among institutions of higher education worldwide. In 2016 Russia's most renowned university, Lomonosov Moscow State University, was ranked only 196th in the world in the Times Higher Education World University Rankings. And the nation's oldest

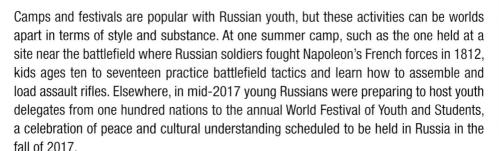

War and Peace Among Russia's Youth

Camps and festivals are popular with Russian youth, but these activities can be worlds apart in terms of style and substance. At one summer camp, such as the one held at a site near the battlefield where Russian soldiers fought Napoleon's French forces in 1812, kids ages ten to seventeen practice battlefield tactics and learn how to assemble and load assault rifles. Elsewhere, in mid-2017 young Russians were preparing to host youth delegates from one hundred nations to the annual World Festival of Youth and Students, a celebration of peace and cultural understanding scheduled to be held in Russia in the fall of 2017.

education institution, Saint Petersburg State University, the alma mater of Putin and an impressive collection of scientists, Nobel laureates, and other luminaries, did not even crack the top four hundred. To help boost the prestige and quality of Russia's universities, Putin launched Project 5-100. Its goal is to place five Russian universities among the top one hundred universities in the world by 2020.

Since 2000 educators in Russia have linked their students with the nation's leading scientists, researchers, engineers, and others in STEM professions. The annual Week of High Technolo-

A student walks near the Twelve Colleges building on the campus of Saint Petersburg State University. The Russian government has begun investing more in its universities in an effort to boost the quality and prestige of schools.

gies features Skype lectures and question-and-answer sessions with leaders in STEM fields and students in their classrooms across Russia. Sochi, Russia, also hosts an annual gathering of students to show off their science and engineering achievements. The goal of this event is to inspire the next generation of tech leaders, astronauts, doctors, and other science and engineering professionals.

Reasons for Hope

New science research labs, modern factories, and tech centers are popping up throughout Russia, all part of the government's efforts to modernize its economy and provide better-paying jobs to its citizens. Efforts are also under way to improve rail systems, bridges, and roads. Better technology and agricultural practices are also making their way out to the rural regions of Russia. "There are a lot of projects being designed now," says Yura, a Moscow State University student. "A path forward is being created. There's no stagnation."[49]

And though plenty of young Russians are looking ahead to a more financially comfortable and secure life, an increasing number of youths are inspiring their peers by focusing on issues of social justice. For example, twenty-five-year-old Olga Nikolaenko is director of the Center for Adaptation and Education of Refugee Children, which helps young refugees find homes and get settled into school and Russian society. She oversees a group of more than seventy volunteers, many of them teenagers. Another young activist, Lidia Moniava, started volunteering with Moscow's sole children's hospice when she was in high school. In less than ten years, she has become the hospice's executive director. The program relies on donations and whatever small grants it can get from the government. Doctors donate their time, but teenagers and older adults are vital as volunteers who help provide social support and a warm, friendly presence to the terminally ill children at the Lighthouse Children's Hospice.

Though volunteering and activism are up among young Russians, many still have concerns about censorship, LGBT rights, religious freedom, and other social issues. Surveys of Russians, including those in their twenties, offer reason for hope. Surveys done by the nonprofit group Open Democracy show significant increases in support for some key civil rights issues during the

Growing Up—and Leaving—Russia

When Russia was part of the Soviet Union, the government severely restricted travel abroad. In recent years international travel from Russia has become easier. So easy, in fact, that many young Russians are not just taking international vacations—they are picking up and leaving their homeland. Between 2004 and 2014 an estimated 3 million Russians emigrated to countries in Europe and elsewhere around the world, according to Levada-Center, a Moscow-based research company. Many of those leaving Russia are young people who are seeking greater opportunities at foreign universities or hoping to find more political and social freedom. This outflow of Russia's youth—including the best and brightest—worries the government. In 2015 the Russian parliament passed a law banning foreign companies from recruiting top students from Russian universities to work abroad. Vladimir Putin described the government's concerns in 2015 when he said, "Acting like a vacuum cleaner, they are sucking students already from secondary schools, providing them grants and taking them away. We need to pay attention to this."

Quoted in Eugene Gerden, "Ban Proposed on Recruitment of Russian Talent to Reverse Brain Drain," *Chemistry World*, June 29, 2015. www.chemistryworld.com.

past decade, especially in the areas of freedom of expression and freedom to assemble (for the purpose of protesting). These surveys also show much stronger support in recent years for outside groups to monitor elections in Russia to help prevent voter fraud.

So there is at least some room for optimism among this first generation of Russians born after the fall of the USSR. Many will continue to back the government unquestioningly, while others will seek improvements in social justice and world peace. For Vasily, a college student in Moscow, the best approach for facing the future may be found in an expression used when his grandparents were young. In echoing the sentiments of many youths growing up in Russia, he says simply, "Hope and wait, all life is ahead."[50]

SOURCE NOTES

Chapter One: The Country and Its People

1. Gregory Feifer, "Former NPR Correspondent: On Understanding the Russians," Russia Direct, February 2, 2014. www.russia-direct.org.
2. Quoted in David Carpenter, "Russian Students Dance with Stars in Their Eyes," *Los Angeles Times*, November 9, 1997. www.articles.latimes.com.
3. Quoted in Carpenter, "Russian Students Dance with Stars in Their Eyes."
4. S. Elliott Estebo, e-mail interview with author, November 28, 2016.

Chapter Two: Home and Family

5. Tatiana Golubeva, e-mail interview with author, December 10, 2016.
6. Aleksandra Efimova, "What's So Russian About Russian Food?," Russia Beyond the Headlines, January 12, 2016. www.rbth.com.
7. Anastasiia Federova, "Russia's Suburbs Lack Charm . . . Which May Be Why They're Creative Hotspots," *Guardian* (Manchester), May 28, 2014. www.theguardian.com.
8. Anna Stepanova, "What Is It Like to Live in Siberia?," Quora, February 14, 2017. www.quora.com.
9. Estebo, interview.
10. Quoted in Pascal Dumont, "Student Life in Russia: In Pictures," *Guardian* (Manchester), September 25, 2014. www.theguardian.com.
11. Quoted in Anastasia Maltseva, "The Contemporary Russian Family: Traditional in Word, Slippery in Deed," Russia Beyond the Headlines, July 25, 2014. www.rbth.com.

Chapter Three: Education and Work

12. Quoted in Fred Weir, "As Kids Go Back to School in Russia, Much Debate over What to Teach," *Christian Science Monitor*, September 1, 2016. www.csmonitor.com.

13. Sergey Klementyev, e-mail interview with author, November 28, 2016.

14. Dmitry Dobrovolskiy, e-mail interview with author, November 28, 2016.

15. Klementyev, interview.

16. Quoted in Fred Weir, "A Soviet Salute? Russian Schools' Quick March Toward More Military Training," *Christian Science Monitor*, March 8, 2016. www.csmonitor.com.

17. Quoted in Weir, "A Soviet Salute? Russian Schools' Quick March Toward More Military Training."

18. Quoted in Weir, "As Kids Go Back to School in Russia, Much Debate over What to Teach."

19. Quoted in Marina, "Appeal of Military Life on the Rise," Russia Beyond the Headlines, February 28, 2014. www.rbth.com.

20. Quoted in National Research University Higher School of Economics, "70% of School Leavers Move to Big Cities," April 4, 2014. www.iq.hse.ru/en.

21. Quoted in Russia Beyond the Headlines, "5 Important Trends in Russian Education," April 20, 2016. www.rbth.com.

22. Golubeva, interview.

23. Golubeva, interview.

24. Quoted in Isabel Gorst, "Russia's Women Technology Chiefs Find Springboard to Big Time," *Financial Times* (London), March 6, 2014. www.ft.com.

25. Julia Ioffe, "Why Many Young Russians See a Hero in Putin," *National Geographic*, December 2016. www.nationalgeographic.com.

26. Ioffe, "Why Many Young Russians See a Hero in Putin."

Chapter Four: Social Life

27. Estebo, interview.

28. Quoted in Scott Wallace, "From Russia with Love," National Geographic Travel, October 2012. www.nationalgeographic .com.

29. Quoted in Andy Potts, "Will a New Curfew Help Reduce Crime?," *Russia Now* (*Washington Post* supplement). www .washingtonpost.com.

30. Quoted in Kate Baklitskaya, "Inspired by Sochi, Teens Take Snowboarding in Siberia," *Siberian Times* (Novosibirsk, Russia), February 13, 2014. www.siberiantimes.com.

31. Quoted in Russia Today, "Fighting Teenage Alcoholism Not Easy," February 7, 2011. www.rt.com.

32. Quoted in Kidsave International, "Not Alone: Mentors for Russian Teen Mothers." www.globalgiving.org.

33. Quoted in Thom Senzee, "It Gets Worse: Russia's Kremlin Targets LGBT Youth Support," *Advocate*, November 21, 2014. www.advocate.com.

34. Quoted in Scott Roberts, "Why Life Is Getting Harder for LGBT Russians," *PinkNews*, August 12, 2013. www.pinknews.co .uk.

35. Quoted in Anna Lutskova De Bacci, "This Russian Christian Youth Movement Is Growing by Leaps and Bounds," Russia Insider, October 2, 2016. http://russia-insider.com.

36. Golubeva, interview.

Chapter Five: Hopes and Challenges

37. Quoted in Will Stewart, "Putin's Youth Army: Russian Strongman Sets Up Soviet-Style Pioneer Scheme for Schoolchildren but Faces Web Claim It's Echo of Hitler," *Daily Mail* (London), May 30, 2016. www.dailymail.co.uk.

38. Quoted in William Stuart, "Russia's New Patriotic Youth Organization—the 'Young Army,'" Russia Insider, May 31, 2016. http://russia-insider.com.

39. Quoted in Jim Dougherty, "What Millennials Think of Putin's Russia," CNN, December 22, 2016. www.cnn.com.

40. Quoted in Anna Nemtsova, "Russian Youth from Moscow to Siberia Slam 'Putin the Thief,'" *Daily Beast*, March 26, 2017. www.thedailybeast.com.
41. Quoted in Deutsche Welle, "Russian Students Committed to Fighting 'Absurdity,'" March 28, 2017. www.dw.com.
42. Quoted in Dougherty, "What Millennials Think of Putin's Russia."
43. Quoted in Daria Litvinova, "Suicide Watch: Why Russian Teens Are Killing Themselves," *Moscow Times*, May 27, 2016. https://themoscowtimes.com.
44. Quoted in Litvinova, "Suicide Watch."
45. Quoted in Litvinova, "Suicide Watch."
46. Institute of Modern Russia, "Russia's Invisible Children," May 31, 2012. www.imrussia.org.
47. Quoted in Get Russia, "From Homeroom to the Boardroom." www.getrussia.com.
48. Mikhail Naumov, "Why Young Russians Live and Breathe Entrepreneurship," *Forbes*, March 11, 2013. www.forbes.com.
49. Quoted in Dougherty, "What Millennials Think of Putin's Russia."
50. Quoted in Dougherty, "What Millennials Think of Putin's Russia."

FOR FURTHER RESEARCH

Books

Editors of Wallpaper Magazine, *Wallpaper City Guide Moscow*. New York: Phaidon, 2012.

Anna Garrels, *Putin Country: A Journey into the Real Russia*. New York: Farrar, Straus and Giroux, 2016.

Elena Makhonko, *Recipes from My Russian Grandmother's Kitchen*. London: Lorenz, 2015.

Sharmila Shankar Meena, *The Status of Women in Post-Soviet Russia*. Seattle, WA: Amazon Digital Services, 2016. Kindle edition.

Ludmilla Petrushevskaya and Anna Summers, *The Girl from the Metropol Hotel: Growing Up in Communist Russia*. New York: Penguin, 2017.

Internet Sources

Central Intelligence Agency, "The World Factbook: Russia," 2017. www.cia.gov/library/publications/resources/the-world-fact book/geos/rs.html.

Encyclopedia Britannica, "Russia," 2017. www.britannica.com /place/Russia.

Infoplease, "World Countries: Russia," 2017. www.infoplease.com /country/russia.

National Geographic Kids, "Russia," 2016. www.kids.national geographic.com/explore/countries/russia.

Websites

Just Landed: Russia Guide (www.justlanded.com/english/Rus sia/Russia-Guide). This website has lots of helpful information for anyone thinking about traveling to Russia.

Russia Beyond the Headlines (www.rbth.com). This website is filled with news features and commentary about a wide range of issues in Russia, from schools and politics to sports and personality profiles.

Russia Today (www.rt.com). This English-language, government-funded website includes Russian news for the United States and American news for Russians.

Study in Russia (www.studyinrussia.ru/en). This handy guide answers a lot of questions for anyone interested in studying in or visiting Russia.

Understand Russia (www.understandrussia.com). This blog by Moscow native Tatiana Golubeva covers everyday life in Russia, including food, travel, trends, traditions, and much more.

INDEX

PICTURE CREDITS

ABOUT THE AUTHOR

James Roland started out as a newspaper reporter more than twenty-five years ago and then moved on to become an editor, magazine writer, and author.